contents

introduction

An ancient art

Origami is the Japanese art of paperfolding. Although centuries old, it is an art that continues to flourish and inspire enthusiasts all around the world.

The Japanese word *origami* translates literally into English, being made up of the words *ori* (to fold) and *kami* or *gami* (meaning paper). Some dictionaries describe the art of origami as "the making of simple paper forms such as birds" and this somewhat simplistic definition, along with childhood memories, limits many people to believe that the boundaries of possibility in paperfolding – and indeed with the folding of any other kind of material – are fairly tight. But this is not so, thanks largely to great advancements in techniques in recent years.

Many people in England were first introduced to the art of origami in the 1950s and '60s by the Rupert Bear annuals. The illustrator, Alfred Bestall, was himself a keen origamist and he often introduced the art into the Rupert stories. Later, the TV magician Robert Harbin brought origami to a wide audience, mainly of children, who were enthralled and inspired by the simple, stylized figures he magically produced.

BELOW David Brill's origami masterpiece, Sake Box, perfectly mimics a traditional Japanese wooden drinking bowl for sake.

ABOVE Material or paper napkins folded into Pixie Boots or Bishop's Mitres and arranged on a plate in the centre of each place setting will charm your dinner guests.

Anything is possible

The last thirty years have seen an enormous leap forward in the development of ideas and techniques, pioneered by contributors from all around the world, particularly in the realization of three-dimensional constructions and pieces of origami composed of more than one sheet of paper or using unusual beginning shapes such as pentagons and hexagons. Traditional starting bases have been dispensed with, too, on the whole, as unconventional folding sequences have been devised from which to draw often complicated forms hitherto unimagined. As a result, it is possible to produce a representation of virtually anything in origami.

Getting started

Origami is unique among arts and crafts in employing a basic material – paper – that is readily available everywhere and in possessing creative disciplines that deny the use of additional materials or equipment, such as scissors and glue. All you require to start are several sheets of paper, a smooth folding surface and the attributes of patience, neatness and accuracy as you work. Very soon you will become skilfully proficient in producing a whole range of exquisite pieces, such as napkins and table decorations to grace your dinner table, as well as decoratative boxes and photoframes for the mantelpiece – or to present as gifts.

decorative
origami

decorative
origami

over 25 innovative paperfolding projects

rick beech

southwater

To my Mother, Mrs Joyce Beech:
If you do need anyone to blame....

This edition is published by Southwater

Southwater is an imprint of Anness Publishing Limited
Hermes House, 88–89 Blackfriars Road, London SE1 8HA
tel. 020 7401 2077; fax 020 7633 9499;
www.southwaterbooks.com; info@anness.com

This edition distributed in the UK by The Manning Partnership
Ltd, 6 The Old Dairy, Melcombe Road, Bath BA2 3LR; tel.
01225 478 444; fax 01225 478 440; sales@manning-
partnership.co.uk

This edition distributed in the USA and Canada by National
Book Network, 4501 Forbes Boulevard, Suite 200, Lanham, MD
20706; tel. 301 459 3366; fax 301 429 5746; www.nbnbooks.com

This edition distributed in Australia by Pan Macmillan Australia,
Level 18, St Martins Tower, 31 Market St, Sydney, NSW 2000;
tel. 1300 135 113; fax 1300 135 103;
customer.service@macmillan.com.au

A CIP catalogue record for this book is available from the
British Library.

Publisher Joanna Lorenz
Managing Editor Linda Fraser
Photography John Freeman
Design Penny Dawes
Jacket Design Balley Design
Production Controller Nick Thompson

10 9 8 7 6 5 4 3 2 1

Previously published as part of a larger volume, *Origami*

Picture credits: Rick Beech p13; Robin Macey pp11(l), (12t), 14(t&b);
Kelly-Mooney/Corbis p15 (l)

The author and publishers would like to thank the origamists who
contributed their designs to this book: Angela Baldo p7; David Brill p6;
Vincent Floderer pp61–63; Tomoko Fuse p65; Gay Merrill Gross
pp82–84; Larry Hart pp46–47; Prof. Humiaki Huzita pp50–51; Paul
Jackson pp78–79; Eric Joisel p14; Eric Kenneway pp40–41, 58–60;
Laura Kruskal p85; Hiroshi Kumasaka pp86–87; Michael LaFosse p38;
Jose Meeusen pp80–81; David Mitchell p12; Francis Ow pp52–54;
Aldo Putignano pp55–57; Sanae Sakai pp90–93; Valerie Vann p7;
Martin Wall pp88–89; Stephen Weiss pp74–75; Akira Yoshizawa p14.

RIGHT Many folders enjoy the challenge of modifying an original design. Here, American enthusiast Angela Baldo has produced a variation on a classic seashell design by Toshikazu Kawasaki. The use of a topographical map is striking.

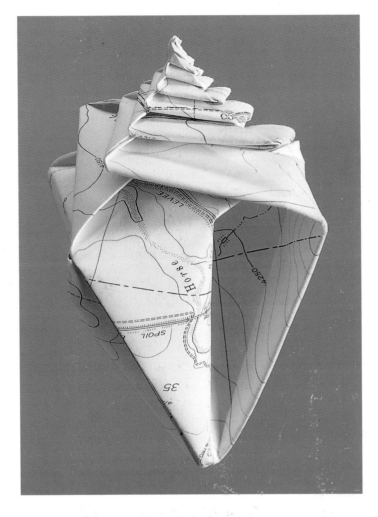

The world is now blessed with a number of designers who consistently arrive at astonishing results from their explorations of paper. One such is the exquisite reproduction by David Brill of a Sake Box, which the creator discovered in its original form during a visit to Japan (traditionally the box is fashioned from a light wood). The unusually shaped recess at the top of the box was created by an interior twisting method, which remains concealed once the box is locked together from the underside. Another extraordinary example is Valerie Vann's Magic Rose Cube, which at first glance is a simple cube but opens up into a splendid rose form.

Whilst most origami enthusiasts are "purists" who believe in origami being produced from uncut paper, some may make allowances for the odd slit here and there if the same result could not physically be achieved without the use of the scissors. Such a cultured discipline, however, inspires those taking up the art to think and rethink their design objectives and promotes much sharing of ideas. Many times various paperfolders throughout the world arrive at different solutions to the same "problem". Whatever your view, the most important thing is to enjoy origami for the beautiful and creative art form it is. Very often the simplest and most elegant forms turn out to be the most pleasing aesthetically as well as in the making.

ABOVE Valerie Vann's amazing Magic Rose Cube transforms from a simple cube to an exquisite rose.

Decorative projects

This collection begins with such simple delights as the Page Corner and Letterfold, two novel but practical ideas for marking your place in a book and sending a posted greeting without the need for a conventional envelope, where the paper that is written on is itself folded into a self-locking letter ready for mailing. There is wonder to be found everywhere in origami, especially in certain little flourishes within folding sequences that are full of surprise and delight: the joining of each unit of the Heart Coaster and the unexpected climax of the model when it is finally turned over on to the reverse side; the brilliant way the handles are fastened in for the Easter Basket; sliding out the concealed portion of paper to make the heel of the Christmas Stocking; and the beautiful collapsing finale to the Star where all the carefully prepared creases swivel and squash inwards to give you the resulting form.

A History of
the Art

With the advent of paper came paperfolding, and

for over 2,000 years origami has been a source of

interest, enjoyment and intellectual stimulation for

adults and children alike. In recent times origami

has also become an educational tool, and a symbol

of peace and remembrance, while for millions of

people all over the world paperfolding continues to

be an unrivalled pastime.

traditions and innovations

Paperfolding originated in China around the 1st or 2nd century AD, and reached Japan in the 6th century. It began as an art which, like many others in Japanese culture, was based on suggestion rather than realism: a few simple creases that evoked the spirit of an animal, a flower, or a bird, for example, rather than producing a detailed representation.

The Japanese tradition

Over the following generations, origami would become familiar in many aspects of Japanese culture. By the Heian period, from 794–1185, origami was a significant part of the ceremonial life of the Japanese nobility. Samurai warriors would exchange gifts adorned with noshi – good luck tokens of folded paper and strips of abalone (shellfish) or dried meat. Shinto noblemen celebrated weddings with glasses of sake decorated with male and female paper butterflies, representing the bride and groom. Tea-ceremony masters received their diplomas specially folded for secrecy; once the wrapping had been opened, it could not be refolded without extra creases being added, which would show the document had already been seen.

When paper became inexpensive enough to be used by everyone, origami assumed a new ceremonial role, as a means of social stratification. During the Muromachi period, 1338–1573, origami styles served to distinguish classes among the aristocratic samurai. In the Tokugawa period, 1603–1867, a democratization of origami occurred, as Japanese art and culture

RIGHT
A contemporary version of a Japanese noshi.

RIGHT Ancient Japanese woodblock showing a magician who, according to legend, folded a flapping bird so realistic that it took flight.

群鷺

blossomed. This period saw the emergence of the bird base as documented in the oldest surviving publication on origami, the *Senbazuru Orikata* (How to Fold a Thousand Cranes). A base is a set of folds, in this case representing a bird, from which other, more elaborate, bird designs could be created. In 1845 the *Kan no mado* (Window on Midwinter) was published, the first comprehensive collection of origami figures.

A symbol of peace

After the atomic bomb was dropped on Hiroshima in 1945, killing over 75,000 people, radiation sickness and various forms of cancer began claiming even more lives. One such was Sadako Sasaki, who was diagnosed with leukaemia in 1955. She had been two years old at the time of the blast, and was apparently unhurt despite being only a mile and a half away from the epicentre of the explosion. Ten years later so many children were being diagnosed with leukaemia that it had become known as "A-bomb disease."

While Sadako was in hospital a friend folded her a traditional origami crane. This was a highly symbolic gift because the crane, which is a sacred bird in Japan, is believed to live for a thousand years and to have the power of granting wishes. Anyone who folds a thousand cranes will have their wish granted.

ABOVE The Children's Peace Monument at Hiroshima, which is annually draped with thousands of paper cranes.

Sadako began folding cranes with every bit of paper she could find. At first, all of her wishes were for health, but as she grew weaker, she began wishing instead for world peace. By the time she died, she had folded 644 cranes; her friends folded the remaining cranes. They later formed a club and began raising money for a monument. Students from over 3,000 schools in Japan and from nine other countries gave donations, and three years later, in 1958, the Children's Peace Monument was unveiled in Hiroshima's Peace Park. Now every year on 6 August, Peace Day is commemorated and people from all over the world send paper cranes to the park.

A Moorish parallel

The Japanese were not the only ones to cultivate the art of paperfolding. It was developed simultaneously by the Moors, who took paperfolding to Spain during their invasion in the 8th century AD. The Moors were excellent mathematicians and astronomers, and introduced the theory of paperfolding as an aid to teaching the principles of geometry. Their activity flourished in the 13th century and the traditions of paperfolding survive to the present day. It was practised and documented by the Spanish philosopher and poet Miguel de Unamuno (1864–1936).

Origami today

In the West, origami gained the reputation of being little more than a child's pastime, and never achieved status as an art. For generations, European and American schoolchildren have grown up familiar with waterbombs and flapping birds, jumping frogs and fortune tellers. However, more recently, enthusiasts from all over the world have begun to recognize origami as an intellectual pursuit, as well as a highly creative and fashionable exercise.

In 1967 the British Origami Society in England was formed. It evolved from the Portfolio Society, which had a privately circulated newsletter. Following a suggestion by Tim Ward and Trevor Hatchett in the Southern Portfolio Notebook, it was decided that a new society should be formed for fellow origami enthusiasts, and a magazine produced to be distributed countrywide among its members.

The early days were very exciting for David Lister, Iris Walker, Sydney French and others, as they began to correspond with Lillian Oppenheimer in the United States of America, and Akira Yoshizawa in Japan, together with other devotees of the art. The boundaries in the complexity of origami creations began to broaden, and, by the mid-1970s, it was realized that different techniques and folding methods could be applied to the paper, whereas, in the past, only designs originating from traditional bases had been used.

RIGHT A stylized Moorish origami design.

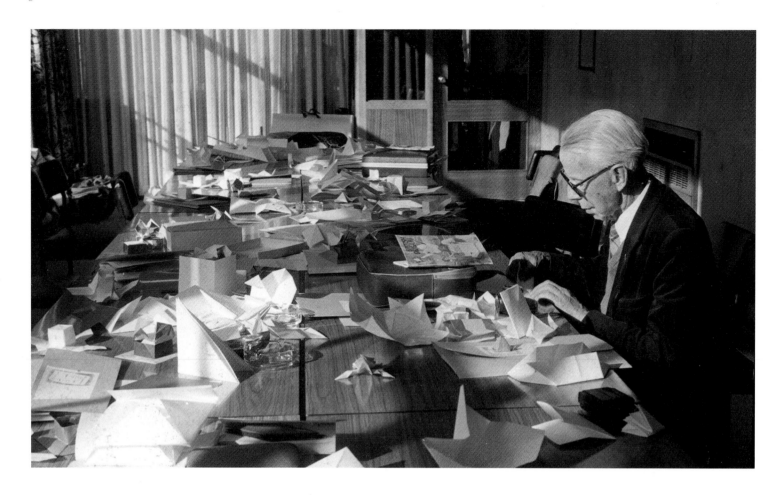

Several milestone discoveries, by folders such as Fred Rohm and Neal Elias in the United States, and Max Hulme and David Brill in the United Kingdom, proved that no subject was beyond tackling where an origami representation was concerned. Indeed, many modern enthusiasts began to create their own bases. This extended the variety of models that could be made.

Elias devised a system known as box-pleating, where the paper is collapsed into a concertina. By using 45-degree creases within these folds, a whole range of animals and human figures can be created. Sometimes more than one subject is produced from the same sheet of paper, for example, a Matador and Bull, Chinaman Pulling a Rickshaw, or a Mother with Pram. Rohm invented the Simplex base, which enabled an action model of a Snake Charmer with Snake to be folded. Competitions among creative designers have also progressed on to new heights: in the early 1990s a worldwide challenge was issued to designers to produce work on the theme of *Alice in Wonderland*. All models, whether individual pieces or collective dioramas, had to conform to Sir John Tenniel's drawings from the original Lewis Carroll books.

ABOVE A fine example of modular folding; this example is by David Mitchell.

RIGHT The author (right) and Larry Hart producing a giant elephant to demonstrate the strength and durability of paper for a television show.

There is still, however, the "less-is-more" philosophy among many folders, due to the emphasis Western origami places on design technique rather than aesthetic beauty. So, while some prefer to fold the working Cuckoo Clock, designed by Robert Lang, out of one sheet of paper, others will derive greater satisfaction from making simple traditional folds and their many variations. Long-standing British Origami Society member, John Smith, has introduced what he terms Pureland Origami, where models are created using only valley folds. Paul Jackson is fascinated by the interaction of light and dark on simple folded forms and adopts a minimalist approach in his work. While it is technically challenging to produce a working jack-in-a-box, it is a different discipline to invent a simply stylized three-fold elephant.

Modular origami became popular in the early 1990s. It is a challenge to design complex origami models comprised of many units interlocked simply by inserting the point of one unit into the pocket of another. The interest and complexity in modular origami continues to escalate, so that some models, such as those by Tom Hull, consist of several hundred units.

From straight lines to soft curves

Origami is, by its very nature, based on geometry – every crease is a straight line. This is a bonus when folding inanimate or stylized models, where the main objective is accuracy. However, for animate objects curved surfaces are the norm and straight lines the exception and in order to create a lifelike model a different approach is required.

The move into fully three-dimensional folding was initiated by the Japanese Master, Akira Yoshizawa. His overriding aim was to capture the essence of his subject rather than simply reproducing all the detailed features. To do this he introduced two key concepts, folding softly and wet folding.

Most origami projects require the folder to make each crease as sharp as possible so that there is either a firm crease or no crease at all. Yoshizawa suggested that some creases should be made more softly than others, allowing a finished model to possess a whole spectrum of creases, from sharp through to very gentle. However, the technical problem of adding gentle creases is that they do not readily stay in place, and therefore the completed works are fragile and temporary. Yoshizawa overcame this by wet folding:

RIGHT This life-size model of a rhinoceros by Eric Joisel was folded for the largest ever exhibition of origami at the Louvre in Paris in 1998. Because it was wet-folded it has a more realistic appearance.

folding with dampened paper which retained its shape when dried. The secret behind this technique lies in the water-soluble adhesive, called sizing, which binds the paper fibres together and provides the stiffness. Damping the paper dissolves the sizing, separating the fibres and leaving the paper floppy and malleable. As the paper dries out the fibres set in their new position.

Only paper with soluble sizing is appropriate, and, in general, the thicker types of paper are best, such as artist's Ingres paper. As a technique, however, wet folding is still shunned by many folders because of the associated drawbacks: dampened paper is difficult to handle and easy to tear. The loosened fibres will separate easily, especially where several layers need to be folded simultaneously. The paper also expands unevenly in the direction of the fibres, so accurate folding is also a problem. In addition, due to the thickness of the paper, it is difficult to make models that require complex folds or numerous layers of paper.

What's the appeal?

Styles of origami come and go, and designers may concentrate on different aspects of the art at various times, producing work of a similar nature, be it animal folds, or modular. If you feel that you have it within you to try to invent your own models, remember that there seem to be two schools of thought among origami designers: there are

ABOVE Vase of flowers by Akira Yoshizawa, 1983.

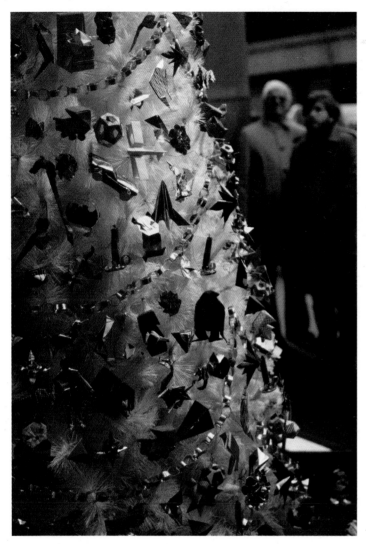

ABOVE An origami decorated Christmas tree entrances shoppers in New York.

those that wake up one morning and declare their intention of designing an origami elephant, for example. Then there are the others who play around with the paper until inspired as to what form it may later take. Both approaches can be equally exciting and satisfying.

Children love origami, so you will find it an invaluable skill when amusing the young. For the commuter and long-distance traveller, it is a great way to pass a journey, and you will find that if you fold while on a bus, a train, or when flying, it is not long before you have a transfixed audience. There is also much fun to be had in preparing practical origami for parties and other functions, and your guests will be impressed with your skill and dexterity.

Included in this volume are practical origami that can actually be put to use or given to friends and family as beautiful gifts. I hope you enjoy my selection.

HOW TO USE THIS BOOK

Start at the beginning, and give yourself time to become familiar with all you need to know in preparation for model making. This includes studying the following sections on Techniques and Base Folds. Only when you have learned these procedures thoroughly can you confidently start making the designs in this book to a standard that will please and satisfy you. While you are folding, consider what is commonly known as the Look Ahead rule: when you are following individual illustrations, it is always wise to look two to three steps ahead, to see how things should turn out. Sometimes, even turn to the final steps for any particular model you might be folding, so that you can see the completed project; this will encourage you enormously. Do not allow yourself to become discouraged; persevere, try and try again, take your time, and enjoy your folding.

RIGHT A string of 1,000 cranes folded by members of the British Origami Society.

Paper, Techniques & Base Folds

Before you begin folding the models that appear in

this book, it is essential that you first become

familiar with the properties of certain papers and

recognize the importance of folding accurately.

You will also need to acquire a firm grasp of simple

procedures and some more complex moves, such as

inside reverse folds, rabbit ears and sinks.

Once committed to memory, these specialized

techniques will give you the skills you need to

produce absolutely anything, at any level,

in origami.

paper

Although most origami models can be folded from almost any type of paper, there are certain designs that beg for the use of specialist material, whether purely for aesthetic beauty, or because of the weight and thickness of the chosen medium. A wide variety of interesting and unusual papers can now be purchased from gift shops, stationers and specialist shops alike, or even found around the home. Enjoy experimenting with different types of paper.

Duo paper

Paper with a different colour on the reverse side is a great asset to origami enthusiasts, as it helps provide areas of alternate colour to finished models. Available in pre-cut specialist packs, you can now find such paper in standard-size packs and even in rolls. Look out for paper that is described as 'fadeless duo' and is sold as art material.

Specialist origami paper

Pre-cut packs of multi-coloured origami paper, available in a wide variety of sizes, colours and patterns, are not that easy to find locally. Thankfully, origami societies around the world have an excellent mailing service supplying different types and sizes of paper, as do a number of specialist suppliers. This kind of paper is fairly flimsy, yet will crease well, so it is ideal for practising your models, although you may prefer to use a different material once you have mastered a particular design.

Textured paper

As well as patterned paper, there are also many different kinds of paper available that have a texture to the surface. This proves particularly useful when folding animals and other living creatures, as it enhances the realism of the subject. Such papers as elephant hide, Ingres and watercolour can also be ideal wet folding mediums.

Metallic, foil, opaque & shiny papers

These are some of the more difficult materials to work with, but if you persevere the results can look spectacular. Paper-backed foil is widely available, and this material has the property of being able to be curved and moulded. Care must be taken, however, as some foil papers, thin plastic materials and opaque paper can be quite difficult to crease well, and reversed creases can crack, whiten or even split.

Patterned paper

Gift wrap can be wonderful paper to fold with, as it is often quite sturdy (medium weight) and nowadays there is so much choice around. Look out for musical manuscript, swirling watermark-patterned paper, wood grain appearance and abstract gold, black and silver colourings in gift shops and the larger department stores.

Washi & other handmade paper

In specialist paper shops you can buy Japanese washi paper, which is a soft, fibred material. This and other handmade papers from around the world give lighter creases to your folding and a softer, less angular look to final models.

Materials from around the home

Before you go searching for special or expensive paper to fold with, remember that your home may be already a great source of folding material. Copy paper, napkins, spare wallpaper, index cards, bank notes (those foreign currencies saved from holiday expeditions), and even magazines or newspapers can be used to make interesting and practical origami models.

equipment and preparation

There are very few essential origami tools to purchase, or preparation techniques to learn. However, it is worth familiarizing yourself with tools you might need, many of which, such as scissors and rulers, are household items, and making sure that they are within reach before you begin folding.

spray adhesive

guillotine

self-heal cutting

pencil

metal ruler

craft knife

scissors

Equipment

Although plenty of origami models can be made with nothing more than a piece of paper and a pair of hands, there are a few pieces of equipment that are essential to a dedicated origamist. Spray adhesive is useful for sticking two sheets of different-coloured or textured paper together, but always follow the safety instructions. A guillotine is a worthwhile investment if you are practising origami on a regular basis. They come in a variety of sizes and a range of prices and have the advantage of cutting a very straight edge. A cutting knife is a very useful tool as its extremely sharp blade makes cutting through any thickness of paper simple. Always use a metal ruler when working with a craft knife and rest the paper on a self-healing cutting mat. This will not only protect the work surface, but will also prevent slipping and thus accidental cuts, as well as extending the life of the blade. A sturdy pair of paper scissors can often be just as effective as any other cutting tool, but make sure that you draw a faint, accurate pencil line on the paper before you start to cut.

Using a guillotine

Often you will require a specific size of paper, and a guillotine is a great help here, particularly as you can align your paper with the straight measured edge to ensure that you make a cut that is at right angles to the straight edge. It is possible to cut two or three sheets at a time, but you will get a cleaner cut if you only cut one sheet at a time.

1 Place one edge of the paper flush with the ruled edge of the guillotine.

2 Holding the paper in place with one hand, use your other hand to slide the cutting blade across it, making a clean accurate cut.

Spray mounting

Spray mounting two sheets of paper together, back to back, is a useful technique for thickening an existing outer paper for a certain project, or for providing a chosen combination of colours. Spray mounting foil paper to tissue paper yields a material that can be shaped and moulded, curved and sculptured more easily than conventional paper, while the tissue paper gives a more realistic look to living creatures.

2 Carefully place the reverse side of the second sheet (the side you do not wish to be visible) on top of the upturned sticky first sheet. The second sheet should ideally be slightly smaller than the first, so that a thin border will appear around the edges of this second sheet.

4 With a craft knife and ruler, or with a guillotine, trim off the excess paper around the edges.

SAFETY

As with all aerosols, it is important to read the instructions on the spray adhesive can and follow them closely. If possible, use the spray outside and wear a mask. Otherwise, make sure that you are in a well-ventilated area and that you have protected the surfaces around you. Newspaper and cardboard offer cheap and effective protection.

1 Protect your worksurface with newspaper. Select two sheets of paper, and lay one face down on your spraying surface. Using spray adhesive, spray a fine mist evenly across the paper.

3 Carefully smooth out any wrinkles or creases in the back-coated layers by running your hand over the upper surface, pressing firmly as you go.

techniques and tips

Although you are probably keen to get started on the projects, read this section first so that you understand the standard techniques and basic procedures before you make a model. Learning how to fold your paper correctly, and familiarizing yourself with the photograph step instructions are key stages to successful models. The more you practise folding the basic techniques the more you will enjoy making origami.

How to fold

The first golden rule is to have something smooth and flat to use as your folding surface, preferably of a larger area than the sheet of paper that you are going to fold. The second is to make all the creases in the paper, by folding in a direction away from you, taking the edge or corner nearest to you and folding bottom to top. This is simply to make the folding easier, and to give you more control over the paper than if you tried to bring the upper edge or corner towards you or by folding side to side.

Wherever possible, the photographs will follow a natural folding sequence so that you will not need to alter the position or orientation of the paper in order to fold away from you. Always make firm, sharp creases. The neater and sharper you make the creases, the better the finished model will appear. Do not hurry to finish the model. Relax, take care and enjoy what you are folding. Do not be discouraged if your first attempt ends in disappointment, because you have not been able to complete the model. If it is not as well folded as the illustration suggests, just try again.

Ways to fold

Technically, there are only two actual ways to fold: either a valley fold, where a corner, edge or flap will remain to the front and in sight; or a mountain fold, taking a portion of the paper behind the rest of the model and out of sight. All other folds are variations of the valley and mountain folds.

Valley fold

1 Fold the lower edge of the paper upward, to an arbitrary point. Hold the fold in place with one hand, and smooth out the crease with the other hand.

2 This is a valley (or forward) fold.

Mountain fold

1 With fingers and thumbs at the ends of the crease you intend to make, fold the paper behind, pinching in the fold. Here, the fold is made to a corner.

2 Smooth out the crease. This is a mountain (or backward) fold.

Pre-crease

Often you will fold and unfold the paper in order to leave a crease which will act as a guideline for a later definite fold. This is called a pre-crease.

Pinch crease

1 Sometimes when you are making a crease, you do not actually want to crease through every layer of paper, or even all the way across the paper, but wish to make a tiny mark or short crease line to act as a guide for a later definite fold. To do this, simply apply pressure to a part of the fold.

2 Unfold, leaving a small crease mark as your guide.

Dividing into thirds

Often you will need to be able to fold the paper accurately into three equal parts or thirds. This procedure is a little experimental, so take your time and fold carefully.

1 Using a rectangular sheet of paper, and with the shorter sides horizontal, fold the lower edge upward, to a point which you judge to be one-third of the way down from the upper edge. Make a very soft crease.

2 Fold the upper edge down over the section of paper folded in step 1. Make a soft crease. Unfold the paper. If you have estimated the flap in step 1 correctly, you should now have three horizontal borders of equal depth. Each outer raw edge could then be folded inward, and would meet with one of the creases made in steps 1–2. If you are slightly out in your estimation, then try again, making the initial crease slightly higher or lower than before.

Pleat fold

This is the concertina effect produced when a flap is doubled back on itself.

1 Make two parallel valley folds in a sheet of paper. Turn the paper over so that these horizontal creases are now mountain creases.

2 Pinch the lower crease between fingers and thumb of each hand. Slide this crease and the paper beneath away from you, until you can lie it upon the upper crease. Flatten the model.

ABOVE The completed pleat fold.

Special moves

There are several special moves in origami, standard techniques that are used in countless models in one form or another. Once you have learned these basic routines you will always be able to adapt your skill and knowledge to whichever project you are tackling.

Inside reverse fold

This is one of the most common procedures, which occurs in two basic forms: tucking a flap inside the model or changing the angle of a point.

Tucking a flap inside

1 Fold a rectangular sheet of paper in half and rotate the paper 180° so that the fold you have just made now runs horizontally across the top.

2 Fold the vertical side at the right down so that it lies along the lower edge.

3 Unfold step 2.

4 By slightly opening out the fold made in step 1 you will see that the crease made in step 2 runs through both sides of the paper. One of the creases will appear as a valley fold, the other as a mountain fold. Both need to be mountain folds, so pinch the valley fold into a mountain fold.

5 Pushing inwards on the spine crease that originally ran along the upper edge of the right-hand portion of the paper, allow the triangular flap to be turned inside out, as it is pushed between the outer layers of the paper.

6 Allow the two outer corners to come back together as you flatten the paper.

ABOVE The completed inside reverse fold.

Folding a point

1 Fold a piece of paper into a Kite base (see p.30), then fold in half lengthways along the centre crease.

2 Make an arbitrary valley fold as shown, bringing the point downwards, and changing the angle of the point.

3 Unfold step 2.

4 Slightly open out the two lower sloping edges at the right, that run to the point, and see how the crease made in step 2 passes through both layers of the paper, front and back. Once again, make both creases forming the V shape mountain folds (change the direction of the valley fold to a mountain fold), as you begin to push down on the spine crease running along the upper right edge.

5 Allow the paper to turn inside out, as the spine crease of the point bends backwards on itself and is pushed down between the two outer layers.

ABOVE The completed inside reverse fold.

Outside reverse fold

This move is similar to the inside reverse fold, except that the layers of paper are wrapped around the outside in order to effect the angle change.

1 Prepare the point by folding a Kite base (see p.30), then fold this in half lengthways using the centre crease.

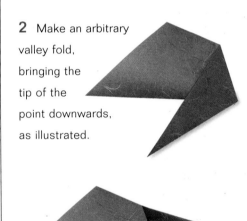

2 Make an arbitrary valley fold, bringing the tip of the point downwards, as illustrated.

3 Unfold step 2.

4 Open out the two upper edges leading to the tip of the point. As with the inside reverse fold, the crease made in step 2 now passes through both layers of paper, front and back.

5 Using the existing V shape of creases, turn the point outside on itself. The spine crease leading to the tip of the point is changed in direction from a valley fold to a mountain fold.

6 Allow the front and rear layers to come back together as you flatten the paper.

ABOVE The completed outside reverse fold.

Rabbit ear

This is where two adjacent edges are folded in simultaneously. As the two edges come together, they are squashed to form another point.

1 Fold a square of paper in half from corner to corner. Unfold.

2 Rotate the paper around so that the crease made in step 1 is now vertical to you, then fold the paper in half once more, corner to corner, making a second crease perpendicular to the first. Unfold.

3 Fold the lower left sloping edge upward to lie along the horizontal centre crease.

4 Unfold step 3, then repeat step 3 using the lower right sloping edge.

5 Unfold step 4. Simultaneously refold the lower sloping edges as folded in steps 3–4, to the centre crease.

6 Squeeze the corner nearest to you to a point, using the vertical diagonal crease. The new point will project upwards at right angles to the rest of the model.

RIGHT The completed rabbit ear.

Squash fold

This is where a flap is squashed down into a new position.

1 Fold a square of paper in half diagonally, then in half again. Unfold the second stage and arrange so that the folded edge runs along the top. Raise the right-hand flap of the model upward on the vertical centre crease, so that it is at right angles to the folding surface.

2 Separate the two layers of the raised flap with one hand, and with your other hand squash the paper flat, bringing the spine crease of the raised flap down to lie along the vertical crease.

RIGHT The completed squash fold.

Crimp fold

This is a useful move for adding a 3D effect or sculptured look to models.

1 Fold a rectangular sheet of paper in half, bringing the shorter sides together. Rotate the paper around so that the shorter sides are now horizontal. Make an arbitrary valley fold in the paper, at about the halfway mark, but at an angle, so that the portion of paper that you are folding comes to rest offset to the left.

2 Fold the upper flap back downwards on itself, making another valley crease. At the right as you look, this crease begins at the same place as the crease made in step 1, so that when you pull the paper back downward, you do so as far as you can comfortably go.

3 Open out all the creases. You will now see that the two creases you made in steps 1–2 pass through both layers of the paper, front and back. Whether you want to make an inside or an outside crimp (see final pictures), you need to adopt the same principle as with the inside and outside reverse folds: on one side of the model the valley and mountain creases are in the opposite direction to the same creases on the other side of the paper. Opposite pairs of the same crease need to be either both valley folds, or mountain folds. You will, therefore, need to change the direction manually of both creases on one side of the paper.

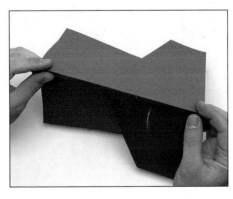

4 Step 5 completed, seen from above, showing the principal crease from step 1 restored. Take hold of the paper with each hand, at opposite ends of this folded edge.

5 Holding the left side of the paper firmly in place, allow the right hand to bring the right portion of the paper downwards. The creases made in steps 1–2 will now allow the paper to flatten into the position shown. Both sides of the paper will appear identical. This is an outside crimp, where the crease furthest to the right is a mountain fold.

ABOVE The completed outside crimp fold.

ABOVE If the crease furthest to the right is a valley crease, then the result will be as shown. The completed inside crimp fold.

Swivel fold

Fairly lengthy preparation is needed in order to be able to illustrate and practise this origami move.

1 Fold the paper in half, corner to opposite corner, to pre-crease the diagonal. Unfold and arrange as a square. Fold the lower left corner and lower edge upward to lie along the diagonal crease line.

2 Fold the lower right corner directly upwards by an arbitrary amount.

3 Unfold step 2. Fold the left-hand edge across making a vertical crease perpendicular to the upper edge. This crease should meet with the crease made in step 2.

4 Unfold step 3.

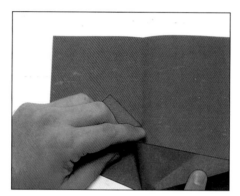

5 Now, keeping the triangular flap folded in step 1 in place, refold the crease from step 2 in the underside layer only, which will cause the paper of the upper layer at the right-hand side to lift up, and not to lie flat.

6 The paper should naturally "crimp" across to the left, where the vertical valley crease in the upper layer of the paper pulls the excess material with it. The central area of paper then seems to "swivel" into place. Flatten the model. The completed swivel fold.

Sink fold

This move entails a closed point to be sunk inside the model. You may need to practise this move several times before you perfect it.

1 Prepare a Waterbomb base (see pp.32–3).

2 Fold the top corner down by an arbitrary amount.

3 Unfold step 2, then open the Waterbomb base out slightly, and look at the model from above.

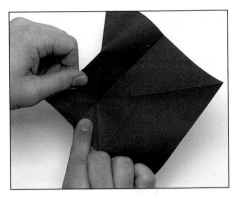

4 In the centre of the paper you will locate a small square, which was created by the crease made in step 2, passing through all the layers of the paper. Pinch-crease all these creases as mountain folds. Some are mountain folds already.

5 Pushing this central square inwards on existing creases, carefully collapse the Waterbomb base once again.

6 Flatten the paper, ensuring that there are two flaps to the left and two flaps to the right of the Waterbomb base. What was the central square has now become inverted into the model. The completed sink fold.

Wet folding

Making origami with damp paper allows you to mould and shape the model to a greater degree than you can with dry paper. Start off with a simple model that you have folded many times before, one without pointed corners and sharp creases. The larger the square you start with, the thicker the paper you can use.

1 To dampen the paper, use a damp sponge or absorbent cloth and carefully brush both sides of the paper until the sheet is uniformly damp. The key word is damp; not wet. Only experience can really tell you how damp the paper needs to be, but if it becomes shiny, allow it to dry slightly before proceeding.

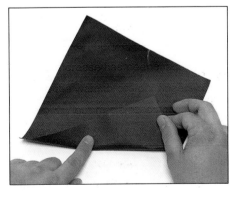

2 Once a crease has been made, you can use the warmth of your fingers to partially dry out that area so it will retain its shape.

3 Continue to crease the paper while moulding the folds as required. Master-folder Robert Lang recommends using masking tape to help reinforce weak areas of the paper (such as where several creases meet). The tape can be removed when the paper is dry.

4 Since the aim of wet folding is "animation" of the fold, you should encourage three-dimensionality wherever possible and keep non-essential creases to a minimum. A consequence is that most of your folding will have to be performed in the air.

5 The feel and appearance of wet-folded origami is impossible to match in any other way.

base folds

Throughout ancient Japanese origami tradition, as well as by contemporary experimentation, certain basic folds, or bases, have evolved. These are standard and easily recognizable starting points from which hundreds of different models derive. It is worth committing these to memory along with the miscellaneous tips and techniques from the preceding pages. Allow them to become familiar, enjoy folding them, and try to understand the crease patterns and formations of each of them, as they will appear in so many wonderful designs. Almost anyone can do origami, as long as they take the utmost care in following the instructions. Do not assume anything, but look closely at each photograph and text caption, until you clearly understand what you are required to do. With time and practice, you will be able to fold many of the models in this book without reading the text.

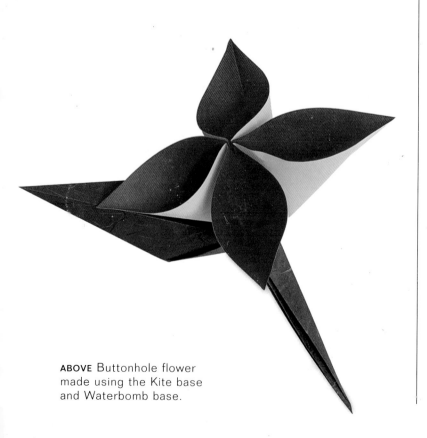

ABOVE Buttonhole flower made using the Kite base and Waterbomb base.

Kite base

1 Begin by folding a square of paper in half diagonally, bringing together two opposite corners. Unfold the paper and rotate it so that the crease you have just made is vertical to you, that is it runs from the upper corner to the lower corner, when the paper is arranged as a diamond, as shown.

2 Fold each of the lower sloping outer edges inward to lie along the vertical crease line made in step 1. The completed Kite base.

Blintz fold

Deriving from a Yiddish word of Ukrainian origin, a blintz is literally a thin pancake folded to contain a cheese or other filling. Because a blintz is folded with all the outer corners to the centre, the name was taken by Gershon Legman and other 1950s paperfolders to refer to the act of folding all the four corners of the square of paper to the centre. There are two principal methods to achieve this, both shown here. The second method is best when teaching origami to children and to the blind and partially-sighted, for it is far simpler to aim for a folded edge than to try to bring the four outer corners to a point within the area of paper.

method 1

1 Fold a square of paper in half diagonally, bringing together opposite corners. Unfold, rotate the paper so that the crease you have just made is now vertical to you (it runs from the upper corner to the lower corner), then fold in half again, bottom to top. This will add a pre-crease perpendicular to the first crease you made. Unfold once more.

2 Carefully fold each of the four outer corners in turn to the centre, that is where the two diagonal creases you made in step 1 intersect. There should be no overlap with any of the new corners formed, and all the raw edges should run evenly side by side to the centre. The completed Blintz fold.

method 2

1 Begin with the predominant colour face upwards. Arrange the paper on your folding surface so that it appears as a square, in other words, with horizontal and vertical sides. Fold the lower edge up to the upper edge, then rotate the paper 180° so that the fold you made in step 1 now runs horizontally along the upper edge.

2 Fold the lower outer corners, single layer only, upward, so that what were the vertical raw edges now lie along the upper horizontal edge.

3 Turn the paper over and repeat step 2 on this side of the paper.

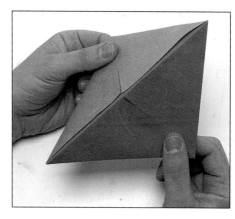

4 Take hold of the two independent corners at the right angle of the triangular form created in step 3, and pull apart.

5 Lay the paper flat on your folding surface, with the blintzed flaps on top. The completed Blintz fold.

Fish base

1 Begin by folding the Kite base.

2 Turn the paper over, keeping the sharper of the two points at either end of the diagonal fold at the bottom.

3 Fold the lower sharp point up to the top, folding the model in half.

4 Turn the paper over, keeping it arranged the same way.

5 At the lower half of the model, you have two independent flaps. Holding down the right-hand half of the model flat to your folding surface, take hold of the loose outer corner of the flap on the left side, and pull it towards you, allowing the pocket behind to open up. As you do this, carefully begin squashing the outer left-hand edge inward, lining up the new creases that you are making with both the upper corner and the corner you have just pulled down and repositioned.

6 Step 5 completed.

7 Repeat step 5 on the right side of the model. The completed Fish base.

Waterbomb base

1 Fold a square of paper in half, bringing opposite corners together. Unfold, then rotate the paper so that the first crease is vertical to you. Fold in half corner to corner once more, adding a pre-crease that is perpendicular to the first crease. Unfold once more.

2 Turn the paper over, and make a further pre-crease, folding the paper in half side to side, then unfold and turn back over to the original side. The diagonal creases will appear as valleys, while the remaining crease, which needs to be arranged horizontally across the paper, is a mountain.

3 With one finger, push down on the paper at the centre. The creases in the paper will flex gently, and the centre will show indications of becoming concave.

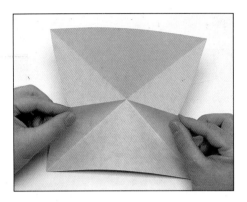

4 Take hold of the paper between fingers and thumbs of either hand along the vertical side edges, at a point just below the horizontal crease made in step 2.

5 Using the existing lower-diagonal creases, carefully bring the two sides in to meet, the sides flattening down to lie upon the central triangular area at the lower half of the paper.

6 Squash the upper layer of the paper flat, so that all the creases collapse into position, forming a pyramid. The completed Waterbomb base.

Preliminary base

1 Using a square of paper with the predominant colour face up, fold the paper in half, bringing opposite corners together. Unfold the paper then fold the paper in half again, bringing the remaining two corners together. Unfold again, and turn the paper over.

2 Now fold the paper in half side to side in both directions, each time folding the outer edges together and unfolding. The principle is the same as when folding the pre-creases in step 1.

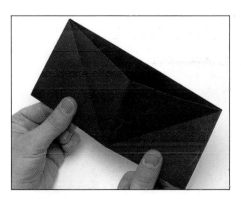

3 Refold one of the creases made in step 2. Then take hold of the paper between fingers and thumbs of either hand, placed about halfway across each side of the paper, as shown.

4 In an upward circular motion, bring all your fingers and thumbs together simultaneously, causing all the four outer corners of the paper to meet at the top.

5 Flatten the model. This is achieved by swinging the large flap projecting upward down to one side, whilst swivelling the flap underneath the model across to the other side. There should now be two flaps pointing to the left, and two pointing to the right.

ABOVE The completed Preliminary base.

Bird base

1 Fold a Preliminary base, and begin by arranging the paper so that the open end, where the raw edges and corners meet, lies pointing toward you. Fold the lower sloping edges of the upper layer of the paper inward to lie along the vertical centre crease.

2 Fold the upper corner (the closed point) down over the flaps folded in step 1. Make a firm crease.

3 Unfold steps 1–2, so that you are back with the Preliminary base.

4 Using the crease made in step 2, lift up the single layer of paper at the lower corner, and raise it upward. The paper opens out, and this corner now comes to lie upon your folding surface.

5 Now allow the sides to be squashed inward to meet the vertical centre line. Steps 4–5 are often referred to as a petal fold.

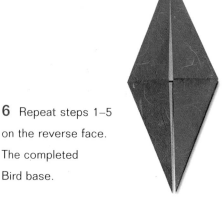

6 Repeat steps 1–5 on the reverse face. The completed Bird base.

Frog Base

1 Begin with a Preliminary base, and arrange so that the open end, where the raw edges and corners meet, lies pointing toward you.

2 Using the vertical centre crease as an axis by which all the large triangular flaps can be rotated, lift up one flap at the right, so that it projects outward at right angles to the rest of the model.

3 Separating the two layers of this flap, place one finger inside the pocket, and allow the paper to open and hollow out. With your other hand, squash the paper down, allowing the spine crease along the upper edge of this flap to come to rest along the centre line.

4 Step 3 completed.

5 You now have an upper section of paper resembling a kite shape. Using the vertical axis once again, fold the right half of this kite shape to the left.

6 You can now raise a second large flap from the right, and repeat steps 3–4. Repeat steps 3–4 in the same way with the remaining two large flaps, rotating the layers as you proceed.

7 With the squash folds from step 6 showing on the upper surface, fold the lower raw edges either side inward to lie along the vertical centre crease.

8 Unfold step 7.

9 We are now going to perform a petal fold similar to that of the Bird base. Carefully lift up the raw edge which cuts across the paper, connecting left and right outer corners of the model. Taking the single layer only, fold this edge upwards, making a valley crease horizontally across the paper, joining the upper extremes of the creases made in step 7. You will need to pinch this crease in manually. Allow the two outer edges to squash inward to the centre line.

10 Carefully manipulate the paper so that this petal fold lines up evenly with the vertical centre line, where the new point should rest.

11 Step 10 completed on one flap. Repeat steps 7–10 on the three similar faces, rotating the layers around the central vertical axis to accomplish this.

RIGHT The completed Frog base.

The Projects

Making models that can actually be put to use is extremely satisfying. You can make an elegant and sturdy napkin ring, photoframe or business card holder for everyday use or as an unusual gift. Or you can use your origami skills to make napkin folds, as well as decorations for special occasions.

page corner

You will never lose your place in a book again with this practical page corner designed by Michael LaFosse. Michael is known for his amazingly realistic animal designs, folded from special paper that he makes himself, so it is nice to see the other side of his work: simple models like this one. A fairly small square, 7–8cm/2¾–3¼in, is an ideal size to use for this model.

1 Fold the paper in half diagonally. The outer colour will be the colour of the final model.

2 Pinch–fold into quarters to mark the halfway point of the lower edge, then fold the single layer at the top down to meet the lower edge.

3 Fold the outer sharp points inward to meet the pinch mark.

4 Unfold the right-hand flap from step 3, and now fold it to the uppermost corner.

5 Using the crease made in step 3, mountain fold the point and tuck it into the pocket behind the horizontal folded edge created in step 2.

6 Repeat on the left side. The completed Page Corner. The corner of a page is slipped into the triangular pouch, so that only the triangle shows from the front.

letterfold

There are many clever ways of producing letterfolds. These are methods of folding a letter into a self-locking form which can be sent through the post without the need for an envelope. This is one of the simplest, and a much-used favourite, thought to have been mailed anonymously many years ago, so that its origins are uncertain. A sheet of A4 (21 x 29cm/ 8¼ x 11½in) or any similar rectangle works fine.

1 Begin by folding the shortest sides together, and unfolding, to determine the centre crease. Be sure that all the writing or print now faces you.

2 Fold opposite corners at 45° to lie along the centre crease.

3 Rotate the paper so that the original centre crease is now vertical to you. Fold the outer raw edges in to align with the inner raw edges.

4 Rather like step 2, fold the now blunted corners at 45° to lie along the centre line.

5 Tuck each of these loose flaps into the small triangular-shaped pockets beneath, to lock the model.

6 Turn the model over. On the plain side, add the address of the person to whom you are sending the letterfold. Add a return-address label or other sticker to the reverse face, to secure the flaps, if you like.

pin tray

Eric Kenneway is known for innovative folding sequences producing simple yet effective designs, as with this Pin Tray, which might also be used as a table decoration to hold party treats. Use a square of fairly stiff paper.

1 Divide into thirds in both directions, to establish the crease pattern shown. If you pre-crease the diagonals first, the second direction that you fold into thirds is not the usual guesswork; simply line up the raw edge with those two points where the diagonals intersect with the first thirds creases.

2 Begin with the colour side face down, and fold opposite outer edges to the first horizontal crease line, that is, one-sixth of the length of one side of the square.

3 Rotate the paper 90° and fold the remaining two opposite sides inward, again by one-sixth, to meet up with the thirds creases.

4 Hold the lower border with one hand, while taking hold of the partially hidden point with the other. Slide the point, and the excess paper, out to the side, then flatten. Repeat on the three remaining corners.

5 Step 4 completed.

6 Turn the paper over, then fold the outer edges to the horizontal centre line. The lower edge is shown already folded.

7 Turn the model over once more.

8 Holding on to the two points at the right-hand side with one hand, place your finger under the folded edge of the rectangular panel, and pull across, until the paper reaches the centre of the model. You should be able to squash fold the paper into a diamond shape. Repeat on the left-hand side.

9 Step 8 completed at both ends.

10 Valley fold the model in half, top to bottom.

11 Lift up the model, and hold so that the longest sides are underneath. Place your fingers in the two pockets along the upper edges, and open the model out slightly, forming the two compartments of the Pin Tray. Allow the two sharp points at each end to lie one on top of the other.

12 Tuck any one of these sharp points into the other; this is quite difficult to do.

13 Finally, fold these interlocked points over as one completed section, resting each flap parallel to the base of the tray. Smooth out any creases with your fingers.

the ellington

This is a napkin ring that was named after the street where the author was living at the time the idea for this book was conceived. The easiest way to prepare paper of an appropriate size is to trim off a 4cm (1½in) wide strip from the long edge of an A4 (21 x 29cm/8¼ x 11½in) sheet. The colour you begin with face down will be the only colour showing on the outside of the finished model.

1 Arrange the strip horizontally, and pre-crease the centre line by folding and unfolding the longest edges together. Pre-crease the vertical centre line also, by folding together the short sides, then unfold once more.

2 Fold the lower edge at the right upward on a 45° crease so that it lies along the vertical centre line.

3 Unfold step 2, then bring the upper right edge downward to lie along the vertical centre crease.

4 Unfold step 3, then add a mountain crease vertically through the intersection of the two diagonal creases. In other words, you are pre-creasing a Waterbomb base. This is best achieved by folding the right-hand end of the paper behind, until the diagonal creases hitting the outer long edges meet. Crease through the paper, and unfold.

5 Collapse the Waterbomb base on the creases formed in steps 2–4.

6 Fold the upper portion of the strip back across to the right, as far as it will comfortably go (the crease will run along the edges of the inside-reverse-folded sections lying beneath).

7 Fold the loose corners created in step 6 inward to lie along the horizontal centre line.

8 Repeat steps 2–7 on the portion of the strip to the left of the vertical centre line.

9 Fold the right-hand end of the strip upward to lie along the edge of the flaps folded in step 7.

10 Repeat steps 2–6 one more time at each end of the strip.

11 Fold the upper and lower edges at each end of the strip inward to lie along the horizontal centre crease.

12 Unfold step 11 once more. At one end of the paper, valley-fold over a very thin strip, while at the other end mountain-fold the edge over by a similar amount.

13 Take hold of each end of the strip, and roll into a ring. When looking from the outside, you will hook the mountain-folded strip over the valley-folded strip from step 12.

14 Lock the model together by carefully refolding the outer edges of the ring (pre-creased in step 11) inward to the centre line. Shape and curve the ring between fingers and thumbs.

lazy susan

It is unusual to find a circular-shaped model in origami, yet this design has beautifully curved edges and is ideal as a table decoration, filled with nuts, sweets and other party treats. Use a fairly crisp, sturdy, square of paper, preferably duo (two-coloured).

1 Begin by having the less dominant colour on top, and creasing in both diagonals. Then turn the paper over, and fold the paper in half in both directions, making the crease pattern shown. The main colour of the Lazy Susan will now be on top.

2 Blintz fold all the four corners to the centre of the paper, then fold each one outward again, to the outer folded edge.

3 Turn the paper over, and arrange as a square, so that you have horizontal and vertical sides. Fold the lower edge to the centre, creasing firmly across the model.

4 Unfold step 3, and repeat with the three remaining edges, folding and unfolding each time.

5 Turn the paper over. Outside the central square, use the diagonal creases and the creases made in steps 3–4, to pinch the paper backwards at the corners. You will notice that in the centre there is the crease pattern for forming a Waterbomb base.

6 Push the centre inward, allowing it to sink inside, while collapsing the model.

7 Flatten the model like a regular Waterbomb base.

8 Using existing creases made in steps 3–4, inside reverse fold all the sharp points inside (front and back), allowing them to tuck in behind themselves. Flatten the model.

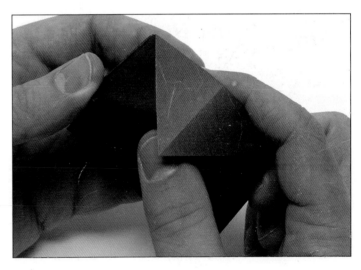

9 Hold the model as shown. While carefully opening out one of the little pockets behind the upper edge, use your thumb to push up on the lower outside edge, curving it slightly.

10 Repeat step 9 on the three remaining sides. Create the circular effect of the final model, and help to form the oval-shaped outer compartments.

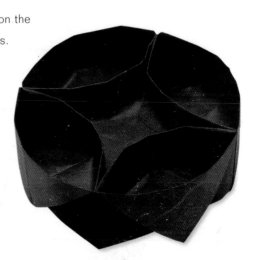

photoframe

This model was designed by Larry Hart, who attempts, by his own admission, to create a "masterpiece" at least once a decade; this is certainly his 1980s special. Use a sheet of A4 (21 × 29cm/8¼ × 11½in) paper, which will be the perfect size to house a 15 × 10cm/ 6 × 4in photograph. Fairly stiff parchment works extremely well. If you use paper with a pattern on one side, begin with that side face down; it will then appear on the corners of the final model.

1 Fold the paper in half, bringing the shortest sides together.

2 Fold into quarters, and unfold. The fold made in step 1 should be horizontal along the upper edge.

3 Fold the two upper corners down to lie along the centre crease.

4 Open out the flaps folded in step 3 and inside reverse fold them.

5 Fold the lower raw edge upwards as far as it will comfortably go, the crease connects the outer angles. Repeat on the reverse side.

6 Unfold step 5, then fold the top point down to meet the crease you have just made.

7 Take hold of the top layer of paper, shaped like a tent, and, grasping the small triangular flap folded in step 6 as well, swing the outer flaps open.

8 The paper will not lie completely flat, so you must now squash the excess paper at the centre, forming two triangles.

9 Step 8 completed; the central area should resemble a bow tie.

10 Fold the outer edges inward on existing creases, made in step 5.

11 Place the photograph, face up, horizontally lengthways on top of the model, and hold down in a central position with one hand. There are now four little flaps which project outwards beyond the corners. Fold these inward over the edge of the photograph.

12 Step 11 completed.

13 Pull the photograph out from beneath these four flaps, then re-insert it into the four photo corners of the frame, as shown.

14 There is a triangular flap on the reverse of the model; fold this out at an angle, so that the frame can be made to stand up. The completed Photoframe.

square box

A variation on the traditional Masu Box, this model is folded in much the same way, except that when determining the position of the folds for the base, you need to divide the paper into thirds. You will need two sheets of fairly sturdy paper, the sheet for the lid will need to be slightly larger than the completed base of the box (see step 11). Begin with the colour required for the final box face down.

1 Fold the paper in half corner to corner, and side to side in each direction, folding and unfolding each time, to determine the diagonal crease pattern.

2 Blintz fold all four corners to the centre.

3 Divide into thirds in both directions.

4 Open out left and right blintzed corners completely.

5 Using the existing thirds creases folded in step 3, raise the upper edge so that it projects upward at right angles to the base of the model. At the same time, raise the right-hand flap at right angles to the base, allowing the corner section to collapse as shown. There will be a small tuck formed in the paper, using existing creases.

6 Step 5 completed.

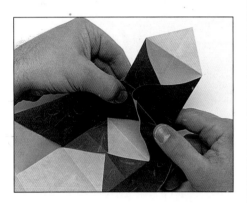

7 Repeat steps 5–6 with the lower edge, again forming the collapsing tuck in the paper.

8 Fold the large excess flap formed by steps 5–7 inward over the outer edge of the box, to lock the model.

9 Step 8 completed.

10 Repeat steps 5–9 at the remaining open end of the model. The base of the box is completed.

11 To make the lid, blintz fold a square of paper. The blintzed square should be larger than the opening of the box by approximately 2cm/¾in.

12 Place the box in the centre of the paper, line it up squarely using the crease pattern and hold it firmly in place. Fold up one edge of the paper, so that it folds tightly to the side of the box. Pinch-fold a crease in the paper, to determine the base folds.

13 Repeat step 12 carefully with the three remaining sides of the paper.

14 Repeat steps 4–10, forming the lid of the box in the same way as the base of the box.

business card holder

This is a variation on an original work by Professor Humiaki Huzita taught to the author by Susumu Nakajima. Practical wallet folds are common, and you might also use this design for stamps or credit cards. Leatherette paper with different colours on either side works superbly well. Begin with any sized rectangle; a sheet 22 x 26cm/8¾ x 10¼in was used here.

1 Fold the paper in half, bringing the shorter sides together. The pockets for the cards will be of the colour now on the inside.

2 Rotate the paper 180°, then fold the single lower edge up by a thin strip, about 1–2cm/½–¾in.

3 Turn the paper over and repeat step 2 on the reverse side, matching up the folded edges.

4 Fold the lower edge (single layer only) upward, to a point approximately 3–4cm/1¼–1½in from the upper folded edge.

5 Turn the paper over, and repeat on the other side. You can, if you wish, make the distances suggested in step 4 slightly different on each side.

6 Open out step 4, and fold the lower corners on diagonal creases, to align with the horizontal centre crease.

7 Refold step 4. Repeat on the reverse side.

8 Open out the centre fold, as shown.

9 Turn the paper over.

10 At the left-hand side, fold the outer edge inward by approximately 1–2cm/½–¾in.

11 Fold the right-hand edge over to the left, and tuck the corners into the two small triangular pockets.

12 Step 11 completed.

13 Valley-fold the model in half along the original centre crease, and again tuck one side into the small triangular pocket on the other. This locks the model together.

heart coaster

Francis Ow has designed hundreds of models on a heart theme, and this ingenious coaster is a favourite. Ideally use paper with a glossy surface such as sturdy paper-backed foil, so that it can be used practically as a coaster. You will need two squares of paper, preferably different colours; red and pink work very well. Begin with the final colour facing down.

1 After folding and unfolding the first square in half, bottom to top, to determine the horizontal centre crease, fold upper and lower edges to the centre line.

2 Turn the paper over, then at the left side, fold the two outer corners in to lie along the horizontal centre crease.

3 Unfold step 2.

4 Valley-fold the left-hand edge over to the right, making a vertical fold; this crease connects where the creases made in step 2 meet the upper and lower edges.

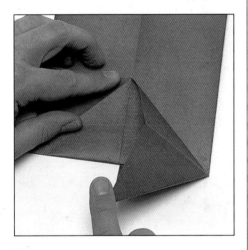

5 Holding the upper portion of the flap folded in step 4 in place, slide the loose corner of the lower portion out towards you.

6 Flatten the paper to a point. Repeat on the other side of the model.

7 Repeat steps 2–6 at the other end of the paper.

8 Turn the paper over. Fold the upper edge to the horizontal centre line, making a soft pinch-crease only through the central area of the paper, just to mark the halfway point between the centre and outer edge.

9 Repeat step 8 on the lower edge. Unfold steps 8–9.

10 Fold both outer edges inward to meet the pinch-creases made in steps 8–9.

11 Steps 11–16 concentrate on one outer corner only. You will eventually need to repeat all these moves with the remaining three corners. Fold the lower right-hand sloping edge inward on a crease parallel to itself, as far as it will comfortably go, forming a narrow strip. This fold should connect with the angle at the bottom of the long side.

12 Fold the upper corner of the paper, now overlapping the adjacent point, downward, so that the short upper edge comes to rest along the outer edge of the long strip folded in step 10.

▶

13 Hold down the larger triangular section with one hand and use the other to fold the narrow strip back on itself so that it lies alongside the lower part of the strip. You will find that you need to make a small triangular squash fold which will form the cleft at the top of the heart.

14 Step 13 in progress.

15 Finally, tuck the loose point of the flap folded in step 13 under the long side border, to lock and neaten the corner of the model.

16 Step 15 completed.

17 Repeat steps 11–16 at the three remaining corners of the model. Turn the model over.

BELOW The completed Heart Coaster.

18 Make another unit from the remaining square of paper. Looking at one unit, two hearts meet corner to corner at the centre of the paper. Lifting up any one corner of this unit, slide the main body of the second unit underneath.

19 Repeat at the opposite side of the first unit, lining up all four heart formations.

easter basket

This model was designed by Aldo Putignano, and is one of a large collection of baskets, bowls and other containers created by this prolific folder. It is a classic to share around Easter time, and looks delightful filled with shredded yellow tissue and chocolate eggs. You will need a square of paper, preferably duo-coloured, and a strip of paper approximately the same length as a side of the square (see step 8).

3 Fold the corner back up to the horizontal centre line.

1 Begin with a Preliminary base; the outer colour will be the outer colour of the finished basket. The closed point should be towards you.

2 Fold the single layer at the top down to the closed point at the bottom.

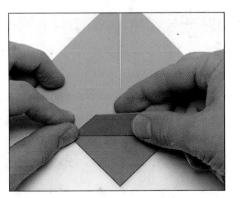

4 Mountain fold the point inside, down as far as the crease made in the previous step. You might prefer to open out this triangular flap and use a valley crease, before refolding to the position shown.

▶

5 Double over the lower edge once more, producing a fairly thickly layered band around the middle of the model. Repeat steps 2–5 on the reverse face.

6 There are two main flaps on either side of the vertical centre line. Fold the top flap at the right over to the left, using the vertical centre crease as a hinge crease and axis. Turn over and repeat on the reverse, again folding right over to left.

7 Repeat steps 2–4 on the two new faces.

8 Take a strip of paper, ideally the length of one side of the square you began folding the basket from. The width is up to you, but if you are using A4 (21 x 29cm/8¼ x 11½in) paper, you might consider using the portion cut off in making a square, sliced in half, short end to short end. Fold the two long edges to the centre. Then fold in half again, so that the handle is fairly stiff.

9 Insert one end of the handle behind the flaps we formed as part of step 4. Push right down, until it can go no further.

10 Repeat step 5, doubling the section over, and locking the handle into place. Repeat steps 9–10 on the reverse face.

11 Double over this entire section again, further locking the handle in place through the multiple creasing. Repeat on the reverse side.

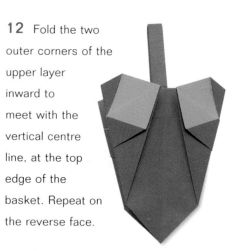

12 Fold the two outer corners of the upper layer inward to meet with the vertical centre line, at the top edge of the basket. Repeat on the reverse face.

13 As you look at the model you will see that there are two diamond shapes close to the top of the basket. Take hold of the top inner corner of this flap, and pull it towards you, making a crease that runs along the lower sloping edge. This will seem a fairly natural step. Repeat with the neighbouring flap.

14 Allow the horizontal folded edge behind the flaps to fold over to the front, squashing it flat on top of the two sections you have just folded. Repeat steps 13 and 14 on the reverse face.

15 Steps 13 and 14 completed.

16 There are now small flaps projecting outward from the natural shape of the basket. Mountain-fold all four behind and inside on themselves, using the edge of the basket as a guide (you might fold them over the basket's edge first, then refold, tucking them just behind the outer layer).

17 Step 16 completed.

18 This now leaves four small flaps pointing upward. Mountain fold these, and insert into a small triangular pocket that you will find behind them, formed by the diagonal folded edges of a previous step.

19 To ensure the base is formed correctly, fold and unfold the lower point on a crease connecting the outer lower corners of the basket.

20 Gently open out the basket by separating the two handle sections apart and hollowing out the final shape. Pinch creases where necessary to give a pleasing final form. Curve the handle and continue shaping the model.

LEFT The completed Easter Basket.

pinwheel and puzzle purse

This variation on traditional themes first appeared in a small booklet of models published in 1972, written by British Origami Society member Eric Kenneway. There is a clever economy in the folding sequence, with the pre-creases all combining to produce a simple and delightful model. Use a square of fairly crisp paper, the colour intended for the outside of the purse face down.

1 Begin by dividing the square into thirds in both directions. Also fold and unfold in half diagonally, adding further pre-creases.

2 Turn the paper over. Fold the lower left corner upwards and across to the right, so that it meets with the lower left corner of the small square at top right.

3 Unfold, then repeat step 2 with the remaining three corners, folding and unfolding each time.

4 Turn the paper back over. Fold in the two adjacent outer edges, upper and right, as shown, using the existing thirds creases. This will bring the corner to a point.

5 Squash the point down to the right.

6 Using what is now a diagonal valley fold created in step 3, fold the inner horizontal edge of the uppermost flap outward, again bringing adjacent sides of the original square (this one and the next counter-clockwise) together in a point.

7 Step 6 completed.

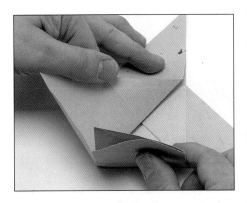

8 Moving counter-clockwise, perform step 6 on the next side of the paper.

9 Step 8 completed.

10 Pull out the loose corner from behind the main flap folded in steps 8–9, swivelling the extra paper into a point once more.

11 Step 10 completed.

12 Fold the point created in step 10 downwards on the natural hinge crease. The completed Pinwheel. This can be attached to a stick, where it will spin in the wind.

13 To transform into the Puzzle Purse, inside reverse fold the outer left corner through to the right, on a crease which runs along the edge of the central square.

14 Step 13 completed.

15 Fold this loose point back on itself and tuck it into the pocket beneath (inside the diagonal folded edge of the triangular area found counter-clockwise).

16 Step 15 completed. Repeat steps 13–15 with the three remaining points.

RIGHT The completed Puzzle Purse.

HOW TO USE

17 To open the Puzzle Purse, take hold of two opposite triangular areas at the sides between fingers and thumbs, single layer only.

19 The open Purse.

18 Pull hands apart gently in opposing directions, allowing the model to twist open.

20 To close, carefully twist the four corners according to the diagonal creases along the outside of the model, allowing the paper to collapse back flat.

gift bag

Vincent Floderer has designed many variations of gift bag, including this one, which has a delightful lock at the top for opening and closing. You might try using fairly crisp paper for your first attempt, but then experiment with softer, maybe textured, paper, for a really wonderful and practical gift bag. Use an A4 (21 x 29cm /8¼ x 11½in) sheet of paper, with the bag's predominant colour face downwards to begin.

1 Begin by having the paper so that the longer sides are horizontal, then divide into thirds by folding and unfolding.

2 Fold the lower left-hand corner in at 45° to lie along the horizontal crease line. Make a gentle crease, as this is only a guide for the main folds you will make later.

3 Fold the right edge of the paper across to the left, so that it meets with the vertical edge of the small triangular flap folded in step 2.

4 Unfold. Repeat steps 2–3 with the opposite sides of the paper.

5 Unfold step 4, giving the crease pattern shown.

6 Fold the lower edge at the left upward on a diagonal crease, so that it lies on the furthest vertical line, as shown. Pinch-crease only what will be a diagonal within the lower central square.

▶

7 Unfold step 6.

8 Repeat step 6 using the lower right edge of the paper, again being careful to pinch-crease only within the lower central square.

9 Step 8 completed.

10 Repeat steps 6–9 at the top of the paper.

11 Fold down the upper third, on the existing crease.

12 Using the diagonal crease within the upper central square, valley-fold the raw edge outward. The model will now be three-dimensional.

13 Repeat step 12 on the lower edge of paper, at the same end. The picture shows the model turned around, so that you can clearly see the box shape formed by steps 12–13. The second third of the paper overlaps the first.

14 On the upper layer of the base, which is the small square visible inside the model, there is a small triangular flap, with a crease cutting across it. Using this crease, valley fold this triangular flap in half.

15 Repeat with the portion of paper lying beneath this flap. By allowing the paper to form a three-dimensional box shape as in steps 12–14, you will find that the layers overlap,

16 Squeeze the front and reverse faces of the box shape together, allowing the two sides to collapse inward.

17 Hold the collapsed paper together at the top.

18 Fold the upper edge down, holding all layers together, by approximately 1cm/½in, or more if working with larger paper. This will make a border across the top of the model.

19 Lift up and half unfold the outer layers of this horizontal border, allowing the central area within the layers to squash flat into the shape of a bow tie.

20 Fold the section unfolded in step 19 over to the other side of the bag, to make the model symmetrical.

21 To complete the lock, mountain-fold each of the upper corners behind, tucking them in-between the layers of paper at the sides.

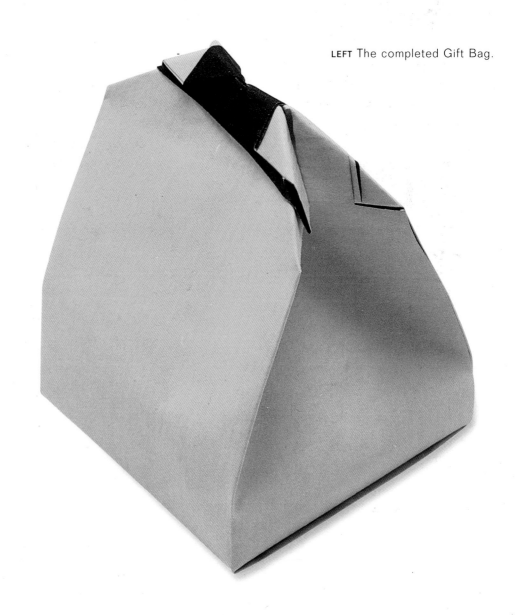

LEFT The completed Gift Bag.

sailboat

This traditional design is also the logo for the American origami society, called OUSA (Origami USA). It is a wonderful model for teaching, and makes a fine place setting at children's parties with the name of each party guest written on the hull. Ideally use duo paper.

1 Begin with the Preliminary base, the outer colour will be the colour of the hull, the inner colour the sails. Begin with the open flaps at the top.

2 Mountain fold the outer single layer at the top behind and down inside the model. Repeat on the reverse side, then flatten.

3 Make two valley folds to one of the sails, the first pulling the point down over the hull, the second, folding it back up again, making a narrow pleat in the paper. This brings the sail back to a position a little lower than the other, giving a small sail and a large sail.

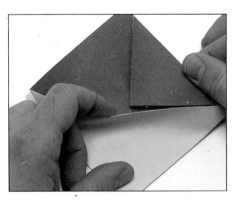

4 Pull the upper edge of the hull out a little, and allow the pleat to tuck in behind it, out of sight.

5 Fold the lower point up to meet with the upper edge of the hull.

6 Partially unfold step 5, bringing the triangular flap to rest at right angles to the boat. This will allow the sailboat to free-stand.

hanging decoration

Tomoko Fuse is famous for designing all kinds of elaborate modular constructions and beautiful boxes with unusual patterned lids. Occasionally, however, she has introduced simple, practical models like this decoration, one end of which can be threaded up for hanging. You will need two identically sized sheets of crisp paper, preferably with reverse colours.

1 Begin with a Preliminary base, with the closed point at the top. The outer colour will be the predominant colour of the final model.

2 Upper layer only, fold the two sloping sides in to meet the vertical centre line.

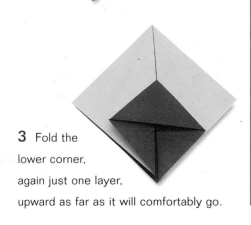

3 Fold the lower corner, again just one layer, upward as far as it will comfortably go.

4 Repeat steps 2 and 3 on the reverse face. Make a second unit in exactly the same way.

5 Make the units three-dimensional by separating the main flaps. There are spaces in between each of the flaps on each unit. In one space, you will notice the small triangular flap folded in step 3. The adjacent space is plain. Rotate the main flap on each unit, so that in each case two sections show triangular flaps, while the others show plain faces.

6 Now insert one unit into the other, making sure that all the way around the model the plain point goes underneath the triangular flap created in step 3. This will happen four times, in alternate directions.

7 Once all the points are correctly inserted into the respective pockets, continue pushing the two units together to completely lock the two halves.

bangle

This is a fairly traditional method of pleating opposite diagonal corners of a square back and forth to create a diamond-triangle, reverse-colour pattern. Follow the steps carefully, as this is a very logical model in terms of where each of the horizontal creases are located: first, the paper is divided into eighths, then into sixteenths on the reverse side of the paper.

Brightly coloured metallic foil with a different reverse colour works very well. It doesn't really matter which side you begin with face up, as there is a fairly even colour distribution in the final pattern of the bangle.

1 Always keeping the paper arranged as a diamond, that is with one corner pointing towards you, fold and unfold the paper in half, corner to corner in both directions, to determine the diagonal creases.

2 Blintz fold the upper and lower corners to the centre.

3 Unfold the lower corner, then fold it back inwards to meet the intersection of the vertical diagonal and the horizontal crease line folded in step 2.

4 Unfold the lower corner once more, and then fold it to meet the centre of the upper folded edge.

5 Unfold completely. Now, if you restore the Blintz fold from step 2 with the lower corner, you can repeat steps 3–4 with the upper corner, making similar horizontal creases. When you open out the paper completely, you will have divided it into eight equal horizontal bands.

6 Turn the paper over. Keep the paper arranged so that all the creases, now appearing as mountain folds, are horizontal. Fold the lower corner up to meet with the intersection of the vertical diagonal and the nearest crease.

7 Unfold step 6. Then, counting upward two more intersections (to one eighth-crease short of the horizontal diagonal) fold the lower corner once more, to make another sixteenth-division crease.

8 Unfold step 7. Then fold the lower corner to the intersection of the vertical diagonal and the eighth-crease beyond the horizontal diagonal (again skipping one eighth-crease to the next). Make another sixteenth pre-crease.

9 Finally, fold the lower corner to meet the intersection of the vertical diagonal and the very last eighth-crease.

10 Unfold the paper, and repeat steps 6–9 with the upper corner. It is easier to do this by rotating the paper 180° so that you are folding away from you. The completed crease pattern.

11 Rotate the paper around so that all the creases made in steps 2–10 are running diagonally to you. Carefully begin to collapse all the existing valley and mountain folds of one half of the model, pleating back and forth as shown.

▶

12 Step 11 completed on the right side of the model.

13 Repeat step 11 on the left side of the model.

14 Turn the paper over, and run your fingers over the model to really press the pleats flat. It is easier to do this on the reverse side of the paper so that you do not tear the raw edges of the patterned areas.

15 Take hold of either end of the strip, and roll the paper into a ring, tucking one end into the pocket created by the pleated sections of the other end. Slide the end in beneath these pleats, and push in until you have a complete, regular pattern of diamonds and triangles.

16 Shape and curve the bangle, which will also give tension to the overlapped area, thus helping the lock stay together.

bishop's mitre napkin

Here is the folding method for a very popular napkin fold. Ideally, use a square, starched material napkin. As a variation on the mitre, you can peel down the two outer points to form a fleur-de-lys.

3 Fold this corner back down to the lower horizontal edge.

4 Carefully turn the napkin over.

1 Begin by folding the napkin in half diagonally, then fold the sharp corner at the left up to the top.

2 Fold the right corner up to the top, then fold the lower corner up to a point a short distance down from the top, leaving a border along the adjacent upper edges.

5 Carefully roll the napkin into a cylinder, bringing the left and right sides together, and tuck one side into the diagonal folded edge of the other created in step 2. In the photograph, the right side is being tucked into the left side pocket. Stand upright.

pixie boot napkin

For this traditional design you might use either a material napkin, as shown, or a paper napkin. If using the latter, be sure to fold it carefully, to avoid tearing the paper. It isn't always easy to find perfectly square napkins, so you may need to "improvise" a little with the folding method. The ideal place to display this model is in the centre of a plate.

1 Fold the napkin in half, lower edge to upper edge.

2 Fold in half again, lower edge to upper edge.

3 Pre-crease the short vertical centre line, then fold the lower edges upward on diagonal creases, to lie along this centre line.

4 Fold the outer sloping sides into the centre line.

5 Valley fold the model in half, then rotate to the position shown. The open edge should be horizontal at the base, with the sharp point to the left.

6 At the "toe", there is a triangular shape, with a raw edge that cuts across the model. Fold the lower edge of the large flap at the right (single layer only) upward, so that it now lies along this raw edge.

7 On the same flap behind, there is a small triangular flap lying above a long thin section of napkin. Valley fold this triangle over, making a clean narrow strip of material at the back of the model.

8 Wrap the entire section formed in step 7 forward, tightly around the "ankle" of the boot, and lock by tucking the end inside the pocket formed by the edges of the "toe" section (see step 6).

9 Curve and shape the main body of the boot, pulling the upper part back to straighten it. Also flatten the toe slightly, which will help the model to stand better.

swan napkin

While this napkin fold can be made from material napkins, a paper napkin works better. As a clever display idea, try sliding the chest of the swan between the central prongs of an upturned fork, which then lies across a plate holding the swan in place. The model is free-standing, however. Leave the serviette folded into quarters, straight from the packet.

1 It is vital to begin with the corner where the four loose flaps of the napkin meet at the top, when the paper is arranged as a diamond, as shown. Fold in half, side to side, and unfold, to establish the vertical diagonal crease.

2 Fold a Kite base. Note that the open end of the napkin is at the top, so it is opposite the corner you are folding to.

3 Turn the napkin over, then fold the two long sides into the vertical centre line, thus narrowing the model to a sharp point. This is quite tricky to do since the layers underneath tend to slide out of place, so hold the napkin down firmly on to your folding surface as you do this, to keep all the layers together.

4 Fold the sharp point up to the top.

5 Fold the sharp point back down towards you by approximately a third of its length.

6 Mountain-fold the model in half along the vertical centre line, then rotate to the position shown.

7 Hold the body of the swan between finger and thumb of one hand, and the neck (the sharp point) between finger and thumb of the other hand. Slide the neck upwards, until it swings into a new position (not quite vertical, but sloping slightly to the rear). Flatten the model, pressing in the new crease at the base of the neck.

8 Repeat this move with the head, holding the neck and the tip of the beak, and swivelling the head upwards slightly, forming a new crease.

9 To fan out the tail feathers, hold the base of the swan's neck firmly between finger and thumb of one hand. Very carefully tease out the uppermost ply of the tissue at the tail end, pulling it upward until it forms a soft point lying along the rear edge of the neck. Don't be afraid to tease out the paper as far as it will comfortably go.

10 Repeat step 9 with the next layer of tissue at the tail.

11 Repeat with the third layer, arranging all four points at equal intervals from each other, and shape the final model where necessary.

rose napkin

The creator of this design is unknown, but it is believed to have been collected by Stephen Weiss. Such party tricks and napkin folds are often taught to the young and passed on from one generation to the next. It is quite a tricky final technique to master, and, because you are using a tissue napkin, you will need to treat the material with great care.

1 Begin with a tissue napkin, as square as it can possibly be (not all packet napkins are cut perfectly square). Open the napkin out completely, and arrange as shown.

2 Fold the left edge inwards by 2–3cm/¾–1¼in.

3 Now fold the lower edge up by 2–3cm/¾–1¼in.

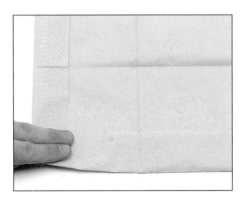

4 Place two fingers across the napkin, holding the horizontal strip at the lower left corner, using your thumb to hold the napkin underneath.

5 Begin to roll the lower edge upward, doubling over the 2–3cm/¾–1¼in once again.

6 To help you roll the entire height of the napkin, use your other hand to wrap the upper portion of the tissue over towards you, over the horizontal roll of material.

7 The rolling almost completed.

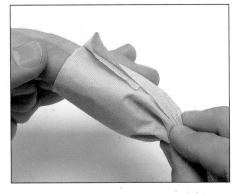

8 About 4–5cm/1½–2in in from the left edge, pinch the tissue tightly, squeezing the layers flat, whilst allowing the left-hand section to remain loosely rolled.

9 Begin twisting the napkin tightly, to form the stem.

10 Continue twisting to about halfway down the length of the roll.

11 Take hold of the outermost corner of the napkin at the lower end of the tube: the base of the stem. Pull this layer upward, fluffing the ply of tissue into a soft point.

12 Continue twisting the lower end of the rose, to complete the stem.

13 For the rosebud, carefully turn the outer rolled layers over, to suggest the outer petals. Carefully arrange the inner rolled layers to suggest the inner petals.

christmas stocking

This traditional model was originally a napkin fold, but has been adapted here to be made from conventional paper. The lock at the end ensures that the necessary layers of paper stay together. You will need a square of fairly crisp paper, not too thick, and preferably with a different colour on the reverse side. Fancy Christmas giftwrap works exceedingly well.

1 With the colour you wish to be predominant in the design on top, fold up a narrow strip at the lower edge. A strip 1–2cm/½–¾in works fine with a square cut from A4 paper (21 x 29cm/8¼ x 11½in).

2 Turn the paper over, then fold in half to establish the vertical centre crease. The strip folded in step 1 should be horizontal along the lower edge at this stage, even though it is hidden in the photograph.

3 Rotate the paper 90° anticlockwise and fold the top and bottom sides to lie along the centre crease.

4 Fold the left-hand corners inward to meet the centre crease.

5 Fold the left-hand corner across to meet the inner edges of the flaps folded in step 4.

6 Fold this newly created edge across to the right-hand edge.

7 Fold the upper layer back across to the left, making a vertical pleat in the paper. The outer corners of this section should come to rest on top of the right-angled corners beneath.

8 Turn the model round so that the narrow strip lies at the top. Valley fold the model in half along the vertical centre crease, so that all the folds are inside. Hold as shown, with the finger and thumb of one hand close to the trim at the top, while the finger and thumb of the other grip the "toe".

9 Swing the toe forward and outward, so that the pleat folded in steps 6–7 is allowed to stretch. New creases will form, and the toe will move position. Flatten the model.

10 To lock the model, open out the two rear edges and look inside the Stocking. On one side only, carefully lift up the border folded in step 1, creating a pocket. Now refold the Stocking, this time tucking the upper corner of the remaining half into this pocket.

11 Flatten the model to complete.

gift tag

Animal models are very common in origami. They are often delightfully simple to produce and even design yourself. Indeed with this puppy, created by Paul Jackson, there are ample variations that can be conjured up just by altering one or two of the folds in the sequence. You will need two squares; the ideal size for a gift tag is, say, 7–8cm/2¾–3¼in square. One square should have a reverse colour, which can be used to suggest the nose.

1 Fold a Kite base for the body. You can use a square that is either duo coloured or the same on both sides, as from the opening folds, the colour you begin with face up will not be seen again. Arrange as shown.

2 Fold the short sloping sides in to lie along the horizontal centre crease.

3 Fold the right-hand point across to meet the two flaps folded in step 2.

4 Fold the upper sloping edge of the flap folded in step 3 back to the right again, so that this edge comes to rest along the right-hand vertical edge to make the tail.

5 Turn the model over to complete the body. Rotate the paper 90° when making the final assembly.

6 For the head, fold the remaining square in half diagonally, the nose colour on the inside when beginning. Arrange so that the fold you have just made runs horizontally along the top.

7 Fold both sharp points down to the right-angled corner.

8 Lift up the flap folded in step 7 (at the right) on the hinge crease, so that it projects upward perpendicular to the rest of the model. Symmetrically squash fold this point.

9 Mountain fold the upper half of this squash fold behind on the hinge crease, to form the ear.

10 Repeat steps 8–9 on the left side point.

11 Lift up the lower corner, single layer only, by a small amount, to form the nose. Mountain-fold the upper point behind to shape the head, and add further mountain folds at the outer edges of the ears.

12 Attach the head to the body with a little glue. The completed puppy dog Gift Tag, ready to be attached to the present and addressed.

pop-up flower

This model was designed by Jose Meeusen, and is a wonderful pop-up for the inside of a card. Ideally fold it from a fairly small square, say, 7–8cm/2¾–3¼in each side. It looks its best when folded from patterned paper.

1 Begin with a Preliminary base, the inner colour being the inner colour of the opening flower. Have the model arranged like a diamond, with the open points at the top.

2 Fold the single layer at the top down to the lower corner, pinch-creasing in the halfway mark, as a guide to the next fold.

3 Fold the two side corners, single layer only, into the centre of the model.

4 Fold the inner raw edges outward again to lie along the fold made in step 3.

5 Repeat steps 3–4 on the reverse face.

6 Unfold steps 3–5.

7 Using existing creases, inside reverse fold each of the corners folded in the previous four steps firstly inward, then out again.

8 Step 7 completed.

9 Blunt the open corner by folding the single layer down by a small amount. Repeat on the reverse face.

10 With the blunted corners uppermost, Fold the large flap at the right, single layer only across to the left using the natural vertical hinge crease. Repeat on the reverse side.

11 Repeat step 9 on the remaining upper points, now in view.

12 Place the flower as shown, against the spine crease of a card folded in half. Stick into place, applying the glue only to the small triangular area close to the base of the flower.

13 Apply glue to the upper side of the flower, as shown.

14 Fold the card in half, left to right, so that the flower is sandwiched in-between the layers. Carefully press flat.

15 Wait for the glue to dry. Open the card, and the flower pops up. The finished Pop-up Flower.

button flower

Gay Merrill Gross has a wonderful talent for designing simple elegant folds, like this Button Flower, which, like the name implies, should be folded small enough so that it can be attached to the button of a garment, as a decoration. It can also make an attractive page marker to a book, or brighten up the corner of a letter. Three squares of fairly thin, crisp paper are required, two of identical size, one two-thirds the size of the other two.

1 Begin by pre-creasing the centre line of one of the larger squares, then fold two opposite edges to the centre. The colour you begin with uppermost will be the colour of the outer petals.

2 Unfold step 1 completely. Rotate the paper so that the creases already made are vertical, and then repeat step 1, making new creases in the other direction.

3 Crease in the two diagonals.

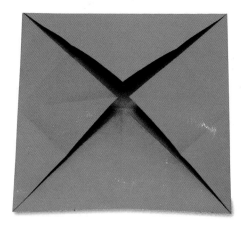

4 Turn the paper over, and Blintz fold the four corners to the centre.

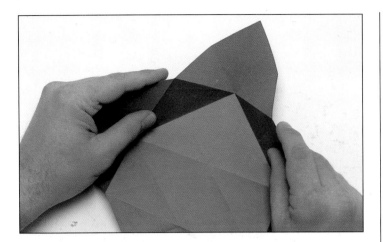

5 Unfold step 4. Turn the paper back over, then fold any two adjacent outer edges to the central creases simultaneously, allowing the paper at the corner to create a point.

6 Step 5 in progress.

7 Open and squash the raised point down, forming a half-Preliminary base.

8 Repeat all the way around the model, allowing the outer edges already folded in to swing outward on the Blintz creases formed in step 4.

9 Fold all the four inner raw corners outward. Outer section completed.

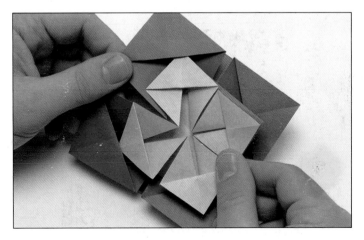

10 Repeat steps 1–9 with the smaller square. Begin attaching the two completed parts of the model together, by inserting all four corners of the inner section into those of the outer section.

11 Step 10 in progress.

12 Step 10 completed. Pull out the four raw corners of the inner section, so that they lie on top of the outer petals (see the final photograph).

13 Take the last sheet of paper, and, after folding in half in both directions corner to corner, to establish the two diagonal creases, Blintz fold the four corners to the centre.

14 Turn the paper over, and Blintz fold the upper and lower corners to the centre.

15 Attach the leaf and completed flower sections together in a similar way to how you joined the two flower sections in steps 10–12.

16 The completed Button Flower. To attach to a button on a garment, slide the button under the loose corners underneath the model, so that each of the Blintz folds slips behind the button and holds the model in place. For a page marker or letter corner, at step 14 simply leave one of the secondary blintz folds undone, slide the model on to the corner via the slots at the back, then refold the remaining blintzed corner as one with the page, locking as previously shown, so that the model is securely attached.

paperchain

So many models look as if they have been waiting around for years to be created; they appear almost too obvious not to have been thought of before. This design, an idea by Laura Kruskal, is a case in point, where two simple units are joined to make the square link of a chain. Other units are interlocked with the first, to produce a garland paperchain.

1 Fold and unfold a 2:1 rectangle of paper in half, bringing the two longest sides together, to establish the horizontal centre crease, then fold the two outer long edges to the centre.

2 Rotate the paper by 90°, then fold and unfold in half to determine the centre crease. Fold the two short edges to the centre.

3 Mountain-fold the model in half along the long centre line, arranging it as shown.

4 Take hold of the left portion of the paper between a finger and thumb of your left hand. With your right hand, take hold of the end of the right-hand strip, lying along the upper edge. Begin to pull this section upwards.

5 Swivel it into a new position at 90° to the rest of the model. Flatten the model.

6 Repeat steps 4–5 at the left-hand end of the model to make a completed unit. Make a second unit the same way.

7 To join units, carefully open out the inner raw edges (folded in step 1) of one unit, and slide the end of the other unit underneath these edges.

8 Interlock several links by repeating step 7 with the remaining open ends of the two units.

heart ring

Designed by Hiroshi Kumasaka, this elegant model can be made as a napkin ring, or in miniature to fit a finger. There is a very simple yet effective use of the reverse colour here, so, if making a finger ring, duo paper which is gold on one side and red on the other would be ideal. Foil works very well.

Experiment with paper sizes for whatever kind of ring you require; the length of one side of the starting square will be roughly the circumference of the ring, with an allowance for the overlap to lock.

1 Begin with the heart-colour side facing you. We are about to divide the paper horizontally into eighths. First of all fold and unfold the halfway crease, then pre-crease the quarter creases by bringing upper and lower edges to the centre, and once again unfolding.

2 Fold and unfold the upper and lower edges to the first quarter crease in each case.

3 Fold and unfold the upper and lower edges to the opposite side quarter crease (now appearing as the second crease away from the opposite raw edge).

4 You have now divided the paper into eight equal horizontal bands. Fold the paper in half, side to side, to establish the vertical centre line. Unfold again.

5 Turn the paper over, and fold down one eighth strip along the top.

6 Turn the paper back over once more, and fold the upper corners down to lie along the vertical centre line.

7 Turn the paper over once more, and fold the upper point down to meet the third crease from the top.

8 Turn the paper back over once more. You are now going to make a swivel and a squash fold. Push upward and outward on the vertical folded edge of the inner coloured border, sliding outwards until it comes to lie along the upper horizontal edge behind. Do this on both sides.

9 Step 8 completed.

10 Fold the flaps down once more, bringing the short horizontal edges along the top to lie along the vertical centre line.

11 Fold up a one eighth strip at the bottom.

12 Double this edge over three more times. The horizontal band formed will be quite thick now. It helps to fold very carefully each time you double the paper over, aiming to position the edge just short of the next crease line up, to avoid getting uneven and messy layering.

13 Take hold of each end of the model, and curve it into a ring, tucking one end into the pocket created by the diagonal folded edge on the outside of the other end. Push in as far as it will comfortably go, then round and shape the model between your fingers; this curved tension will help to hold the ring together.

star

This is a wonderful Christmas star invented by Martin Wall which uses the crease pattern of the Bird base. An effective way to make a card using this design is to mount several stars on top of each other, each offset to the one before, and attached to a piece of card the same colour; this will create a relief effect. For the model use a square of thin, crisp paper with the star colour face down to start.

1 Begin by folding the paper diagonally in half in both directions, folding and unfolding each time, marking the diagonals with creases.

2 Fold a Kite base with any two adjacent edges.

3 Unfold, and repeat this procedure with different adjacent edges, at the three remaining corners. This will give a symmetrical crease pattern, with an octagon in the centre of the paper.

4 Turn the paper over, and fold in half, bottom to top.

5 Unfold, and then fold in half, side to side, at right angles to the crease you have just made. Unfold, then turn the paper over so that the original side is uppermost, and the diagonals and Bird-base creases are all valley folds.

6 Grasp the horizontal central mountain fold between fingers and thumbs. Drag it away from you, until you can rest the entire folded edge on the intersection of the upper Bird-base creases and the vertical halfway line. Press flat, creating a pleat across the paper.

7 Step 6 completed.

8 Rotate the paper, so that the pleat made in step 6 is now vertical, and the thinner portion of the paper lies to the right. Again, grasp the horizontal crease across the centre of the paper, sliding it once more away from you, until you can place it down where the folded edge of the pleat made in step 6 intersects with the uppermost Bird-base creases. You will now have a perfect, small square in the top right corner. Flatten the model.

9 From now on, we only use existing creases. Starting with one outside edge of the larger square, refold on the Kite-base creases, allowing the adjacent flap to swivel and squash into place at the same time.

10 Step 9 completed and rotated.

11 Repeat step 9 all the way around, forming the remaining three points of the star.

santa and sleigh

There are origami societies all over the world, each producing its own magazine. This model, by Sanae Sakai, was featured in the Nippon Origami Society of Japan's December 1996 issue. Use a square of paper, preferably red on one side. Begin with this side face up.

1 Begin by folding the paper in half, left to right, and making a pinch-mark along the upper edge.

2 Unfold, then fold the paper across once more, to meet with the pinch made in step 1. Pinch again, down to about a quarter of the way from the top edge.

3 Unfold step 2.

4 Fold the upper left-hand corner down to lie along the pinch made in step 2.

5 Turn the paper over, arranging the folded corner to be top right.

6 Again using the pinch made in step 2 as a guide, fold the right-hand edge inward so that, at the top, the edge lies along the pinch.

7 Fold the top edge down on a crease which runs horizontally in line with the lower edge of the tiny triangular section in step 6.

8 Fold the top left corner down to the raw edge of the flap folded in step 7.

9 Using this triangular flap (now hidden) as your guide, fold the left-hand vertical edge inward, on a crease which runs along the inner edge. Release and unfold the triangular flap folded in step 8.

10 Allowing this side flap to unfold slightly, pull out the hidden corner, stretching the excess paper to a point.

11 Step 10 in progress.

12 Step 10 completed. This particular type of swivel move occurs frequently in this model.

13 Raise the point created in steps 10–12 so that it stands up perpendicular to the rest of the model.

14 Squash fold this flap into a half-Preliminary base. Also fold up the lower right corner to the inner edge of the vertical strip.

15 Similar to step 9, fold the lower edge up, over the tiny triangular flap folded in step 14, creating a horizontal parallel border along the bottom. Again, release and unfold the triangular flap. Unfold triangular flap from step 14. ▶

16 At the lower right corner, once again pull out the hidden point, squashing outward to the right.

17 At the lower left corner, perform a similar swivel, this time noting that the vertical border is wider than the horizontal border.

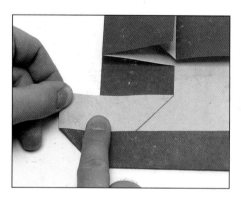

18 The effect will be as shown.

19 Step 17 completed. All edges should be at right angles to each other.

20 Fold the inner lower corner of the Preliminary base up to the top. Also fold the raw corner at the left down to meet the horizontal border along the bottom.

21 Unfold the first fold made at step 20, then fold the inner corner back up to the crease line made in step 20.

22 To make the trim on Santa's hat, double the lower edge of the flap folded in step 21 over.

23 Then double the edge over once more.

24 Lift up the upper right section of paper, and fold the inner raw edge of the horizontal border upwards, to lie along the outer edge of what will be Santa's face.

25 Allow the right-hand vertical border to double over once more.

26 Step 25 completed. Flatten the model.

27 Fold the lower edge up once more, doubling the horizontal border over, as shown.

28 Pull out the hidden point (the front blade of the sleigh) at the lower right corner, and swivel and slide into position, much the same way as you have done previously in this model.

29 Step 28 completed.

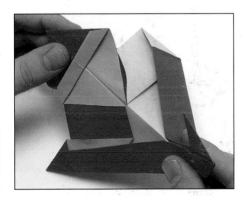

30 Mountain fold the model diagonally in half, the crease running top left to bottom right. This fold is made quite naturally, the thing to remember is not to fold the front of the sleigh section, or the right side (as you look) of Santa's face.

31 Step 30 completed.

32 Add shaping mountain folds to the rear corner of the sleigh, the sides of Santa's face, and Santa's toy bag.

ABOVE The completed Santa and Sleigh

waterbomb

The waterbomb is probably one of the most well-known
origami folds. The finished waterbomb is filled with water
through a hole that is formed at the top. Children love making
them and then throwing them on to the ground or having
waterbomb fights on warm summer days. Use fairly thick paper,
as too thin a material will soak up
the water too quickly.

1 Begin with the Waterbomb base.

2 Fold one of the lower sharp points up
to the top of the pyramid.

3 Repeat with the three remaining
flaps, folding two points up on
each side.

4 Again taking one layer of paper per side, fold the two side corners into the centre.

5 Repeat step 4 on the reverse side.

6 Fold the loose corners back towards you, to the centre of the model.

7 Step 6 completed. Rotate the model 180°, and flatten.

8 If you look at the larger triangular flaps folded in steps 4 and 5, you will see that there is a pocket created by the folded sloping edges now facing you. Lifting up the larger triangular flap slightly, and pushing on the spine crease to allow the pocket to open up, fold the smaller triangular section created in the previous step over and into this pocket. This will lock the model. Press flat, and then repeat with the three remaining points.

9 Step 8 completed.

10 Fold and unfold the upper and lower corners to the centre of the model, making a really sharp crease in each case.

11 Step 10 completed.

12 Finally, separate the four main flaps of the model, making it appear three-dimensional, and hold it between fingers and thumbs with the hole facing you. Take a good breath, and, placing your lips right up to the paper, blow sharply into the hole, which should inflate the model to its cube shape. Use the hole to fill your model with water, then throw.

index